God Made All Things Great

Written by **Michael David Harrison** & Illustrated by **Tyrus Goshay**

MW00897591

GOD MADE ALL THINGS GREAT

Written by **Michael David Harrison** & Illustrated by **Tyrus Goshay**

Michael David Harrison
Email: mdharrison4u@hotmail.com
TgosketchPress
Chicago, Illinois
www.tgosketch.com

The Author:

In memory of my late grandmother, Ida Mae Harrison, my first teacher who instilled within me Philippians 4:13
To my mom, Joann, aunts, Joan, Wilma and the late Michelle, uncle, Alfred, family and friends, thank you for your ongoing love, support and prayers.
To my writing coach, Carole, illustrator, Tyrus, producer, Linton, and narrator, Deno, thank you for putting up
with my boisterous, bold and brilliant self these past few months.
Team work makes the dream work! I Corinthians 2:9

The Illustrator:

You Are Welcome.

GOD made all things great.
He made no mistakes.

From the heavens and the earth
to the light in the sky,

He created the land and the sea
for all to occupy.

GOD made all things great.

He made no mistakes.

From the plants and the trees

to the sun and the moon,

He even added some stars to shine at night that you can see from your bedroom.

God made all things great.
He made no mistakes.

From creatures in the air

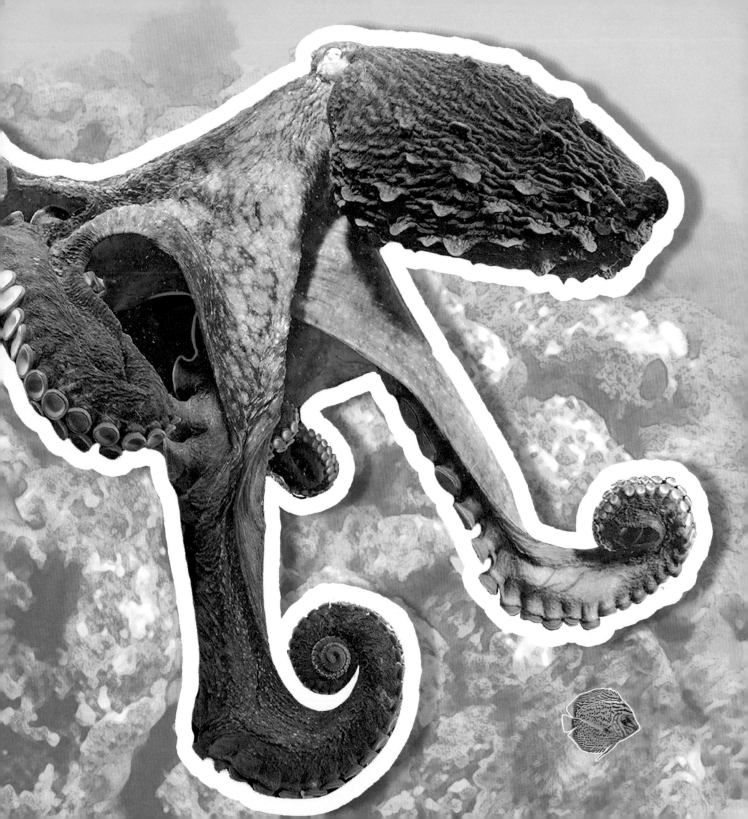

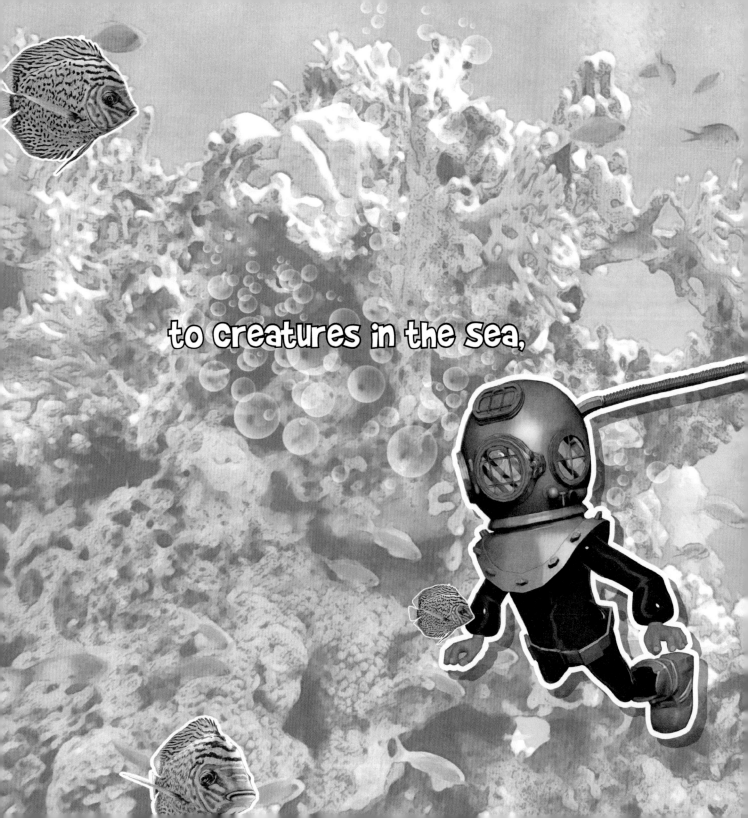

to creatures in the sea,

no matter how high they fly

or how low they go,

He always gives them what they need.

God made all things great.

He made no mistakes.

From monkeys, lions, giraffes and tigers

to elephants, zebras, snakes and spiders,

those are just a few of the many
animals He created to roam the land.
He created the entire animal kingdom to Be
ruled By man.

God made all things great.
He made no mistakes.

From Adam and Eve

to your father and mother,

He created Boys and Girls to Be just like Him and like no other.

Just when He thought He Did all He Could Do...

One of His greatest
creations occurred...

(Tape Baby Picture Here!)

The Day He created you...

God made all things great.
He made no mistakes!

About the Author:

Michael David Harrison has always had a passion for writing since childhood. After working 16 years in the public school system as a teacher, administrator and principal, he has begun a new journey in sharing his love for writing and hopes to inspire young minds toward living out their dreams. *God Made All Things Great* is a dream come true for Michael as this is his first children's picture book. When he is not writing books, he enjoys writing music, traveling and eating out with friends. A graduate of Morehouse College (B.A.), University of St. Thomas (M.Ed.) and Rice University (MBA), Michael currently lives in Houston, TX with a family of 24 fish.

mdharrison4u@hotmail.com
www.michaelwroteit.com
www.facebook.com/mdharrison1

The Illustrator:

Tyrus Goshay is an award-winning digital illustrator and 3D artist with over 18 years of experience. He serves as a college professor, teaching both game design and illustration in his off time. Tyrus has a Bachelor's in Computer Animation and Multimedia and a Master's in Teaching With Technology (MALT). He has contributed to several award-winning projects in the world of toy design and has been recognized for his achievements in academia as well. He also has tutorials in illustration and digital sculpting available on the web.

Visit his bookstore, and see other books that he has illustrated.

www.tgosketch.com
www.facebook.com/Tgosketch
tgosketch@gmail.com
Instagram/tgosketch

Made in the USA
Lexington, KY
03 June 2018